Aunt Happy's Garden

ISBN 978-0-9949953-0-8

Edited by: Warren Coughlin

Dedicated to:
Joyce Coughlin (Aunt Happy) my mother-in-law who took a deep breath when things got tough and focused on the good things instead.

Inspired by:
Warren Coughlin's eulogy to his mom *"Joyce Coughlin's 11 Keys to Happiness"*
Laura Fraser Matthews my sister-in-law who's ability to remain positive and enthusiastic no matter what was inspiring.

Both *Joyce* and *Laura* passed away from cancer but each remained positive and happy to the end. I am so grateful for having had them in my life.

Thank you to:
My husband *Warren Coughlin* for his encouragement and support in helping me write and produce this book.
My daughter *Aiyana Coughlin* for her insight and input on how the characters should be illustrated.

Aunt Happy sees a boy looking sad in some way.
So she asks him, "Dear, how are you feeling today?"

"I'm sad," said the boy, "we've moved far away.
I have no friends so I can't play."

"I too can feel sad, and that's really okay, but
I make a choice to be happy each day."

"I don't understand how you choose to be glad,
when something happens to make you feel sad."

"I take a deep breath and then blow it out, so I relax and that feeling goes out."

"I try to find something to think in my head; something that's good, so I'm happy instead."

"For me, it's my garden and smelling the flowers.
It's such a joy, I can stay there for hours."

"May I invite you to try it my way.
Spend time in my garden, if your mom says okay."

His mom said "Okay", so he starts 'round the back.
He then sees a snail whose shell has a crack.

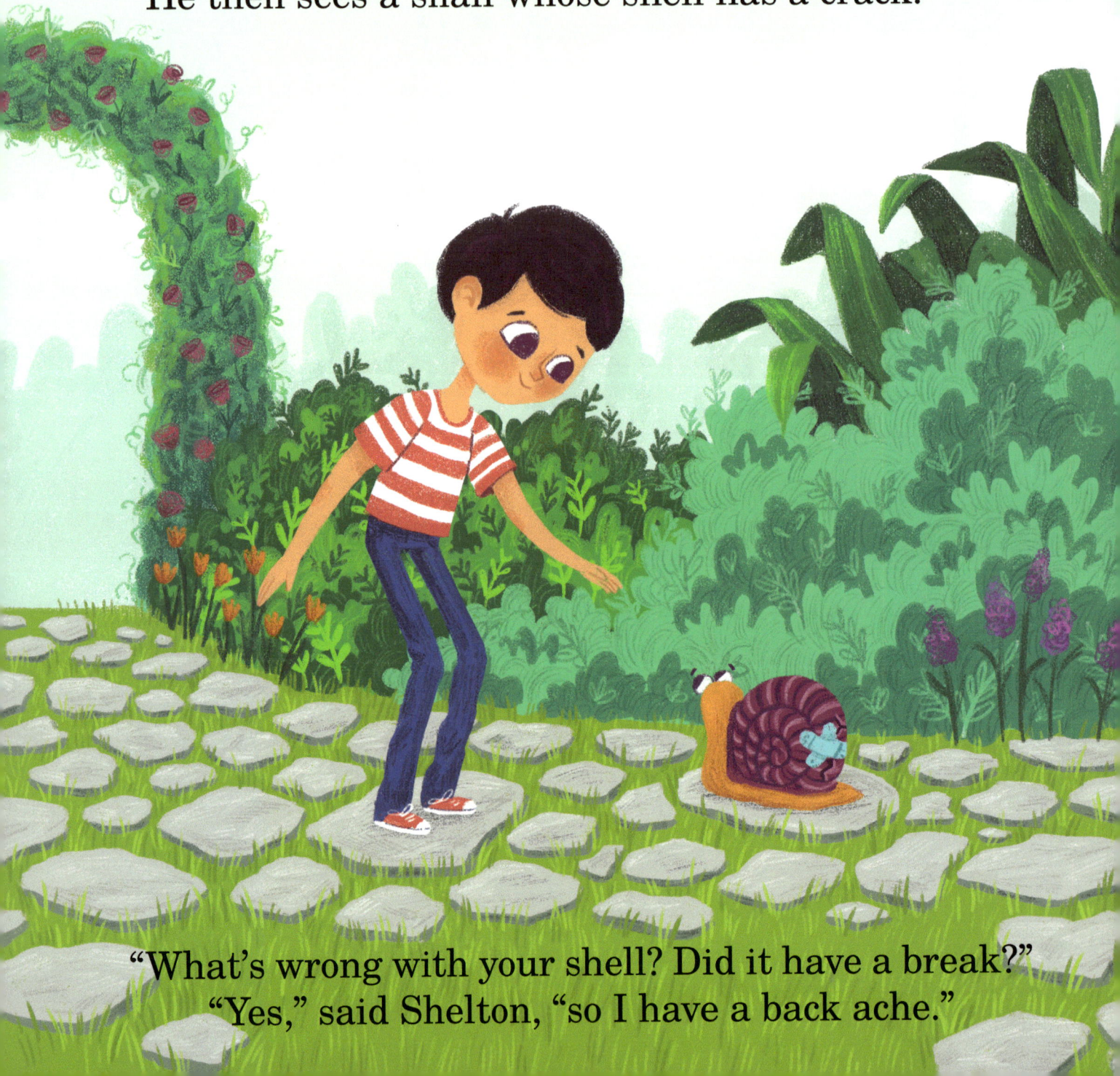

"What's wrong with your shell? Did it have a break?"
"Yes," said Shelton, "so I have a back ache."

"I felt bad at first and that's really okay.
But now I will choose to be happy today."

"How do you choose now to be glad?
You just said you were feeling quite bad."

"I take a deep breath and then blow it out. So I relax and that feeling goes out."

"I try to find something to think in my head; something that's good, so I'm happy instead."

"I think of Slink the best friend I've got.
He fixed my shell, which helped me a lot."

"I feel very happy that Slink is my friend.
I know he will help me each day 'til I mend."

"That's great," said the boy, "that you have your friend,"
as he waves goodbye and walks 'round the bend.

He then sees a frog jumping up and then down.

"Splash" goes the water and the frog has a frown.

Said the boy to the frog, "Are you hurt in some way."
Said Rubert the frog, "Just my pride, I would say."

"I do feel embarrassed and that's okay. But now I will choose to be happy today."

"How do you choose to now be okay, when you're embarrassed I just heard you say?"

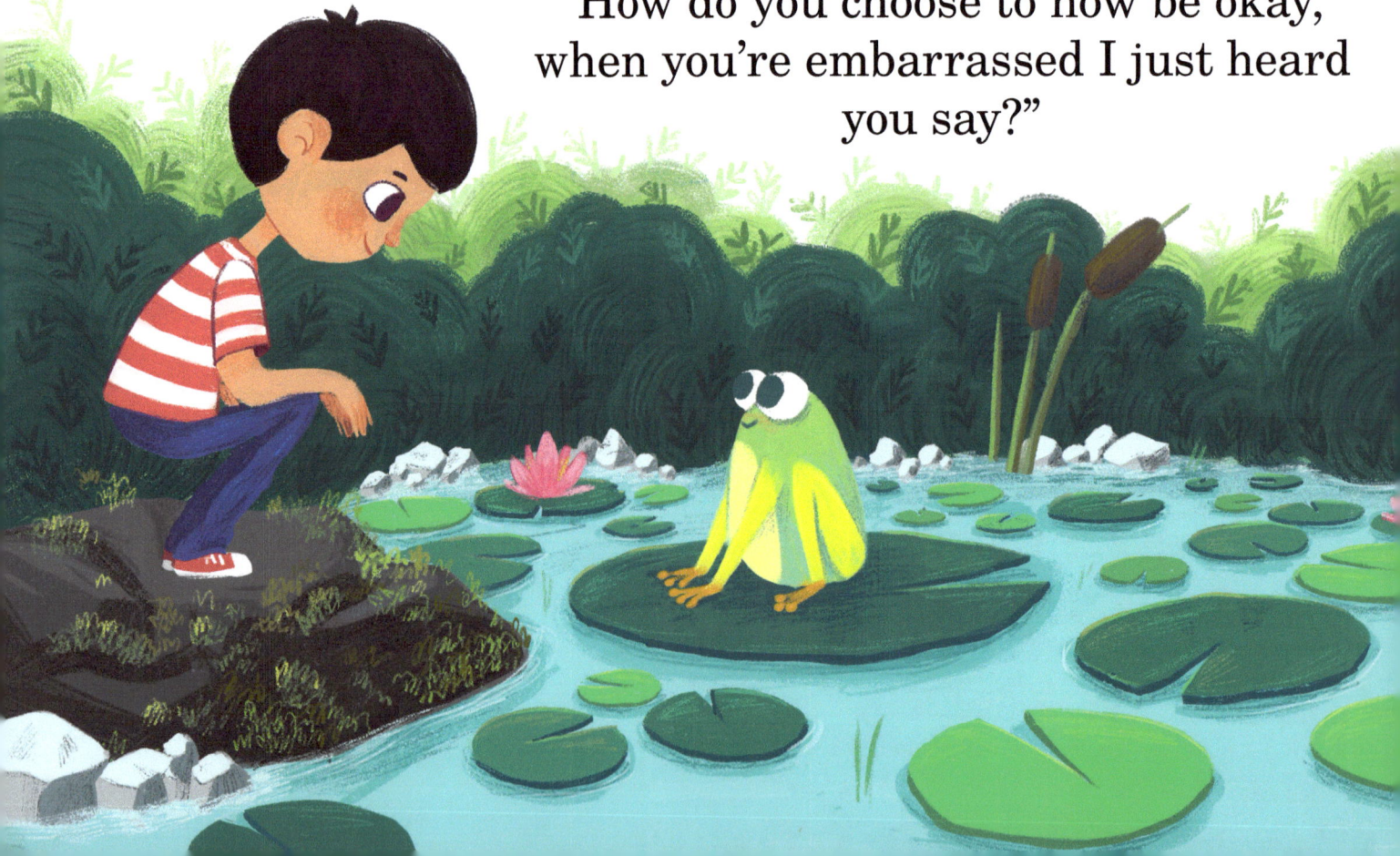

"I take a deep breath and then blow it out. So I relax and that feeling goes out."

"I try to find something to think in my head; something that's good, so I'm happy instead."

Rubert asks the boy where the lily pad went.
The boy starts to giggle, "It's there on your head."

The frog giggles too, "I like when I laugh.
That was quite funny when I took a wet bath."

"Mom says to practice, if I fall that's okay.
I should take it as fun and continue to play.
That's how you learn to get better at things.
Then you enjoy the success that it brings."

"Makes sense" said the boy, "and it sure looks like
fun. And if you get wet you can dry in the sun."

He then hears a voice say, "Oh what a pain. I really can't help I'm as long as a train."

The boy sees a centipede kick at the dirt. "What's wrong," says the boy, "have your feelings been hurt."

"The other bugs say I can't play their game.
I have so many legs that I'm not the same."
"It seems unfair and that makes me quite mad.
But today I would really rather feel glad."

"So, I'll take a deep breath and then blow it out. So, I relax and that feeling goes out."
"I'll try to find something to think in my head; something that's good, so I'm happy instead."

"I'm most happy when I do my train dance." Peedy's legs start to move into a prance.

CHOO CHOO CHOO

He then starts to hop and sings his train song. "Choo choo choo" he sings, as he moves along.

The other bugs see him having great fun.
They stop their game, though no one has won.

They say "Can we join your train and your song?"
"Yes, that makes me happy, as now I belong."

Continuing down the path of the garden,
he hears an "Oh Dear" and says "Beg your pardon."

Says the boy to a sunflower "Are you feeling okay?"
You look rather worried about something I'd say."

"I am rather worried, as my friends all grow tall.
But then look at me. I'm not growing at all."

"Oh, I wish I had sunflower seeds too.
But I don't have any. Oh what will I do?"

Said the boy, "Well, I have heard you can choose to be glad. Even if you're worried and feeling quite bad."

First take a deep breath and then blow it out. So you relax and that feeling goes out.

"Then try to find something to think in your head; something that's good, so you're happy instead."

"It makes me happy to look at the sun.
The warmth is relaxing and the worry is done."
Flo put on sunglasses and looked at the sun.
Then began to grow taller as the boy looked on.

"Look, I'm growing. I feel great I'd say.
Thanks. You helped me to be happy today."

The boy then reaches the end of the path.
He sees Aunt Happy by the bird bath.

"Hi Aunt Happy" said the boy with a smile, "I've been in your garden for quite a long while."

"I can tell by your smile that you had a good time.
You must have met some good friends of mine."

"I did meet your friends and now I know why,
it's best to choose happy over wanting to cry.
If you focus on positive things in your day, then
it just seems good things come your way."

"So, now I'll find something to think in my head;
something that's good, so I'm happy instead."

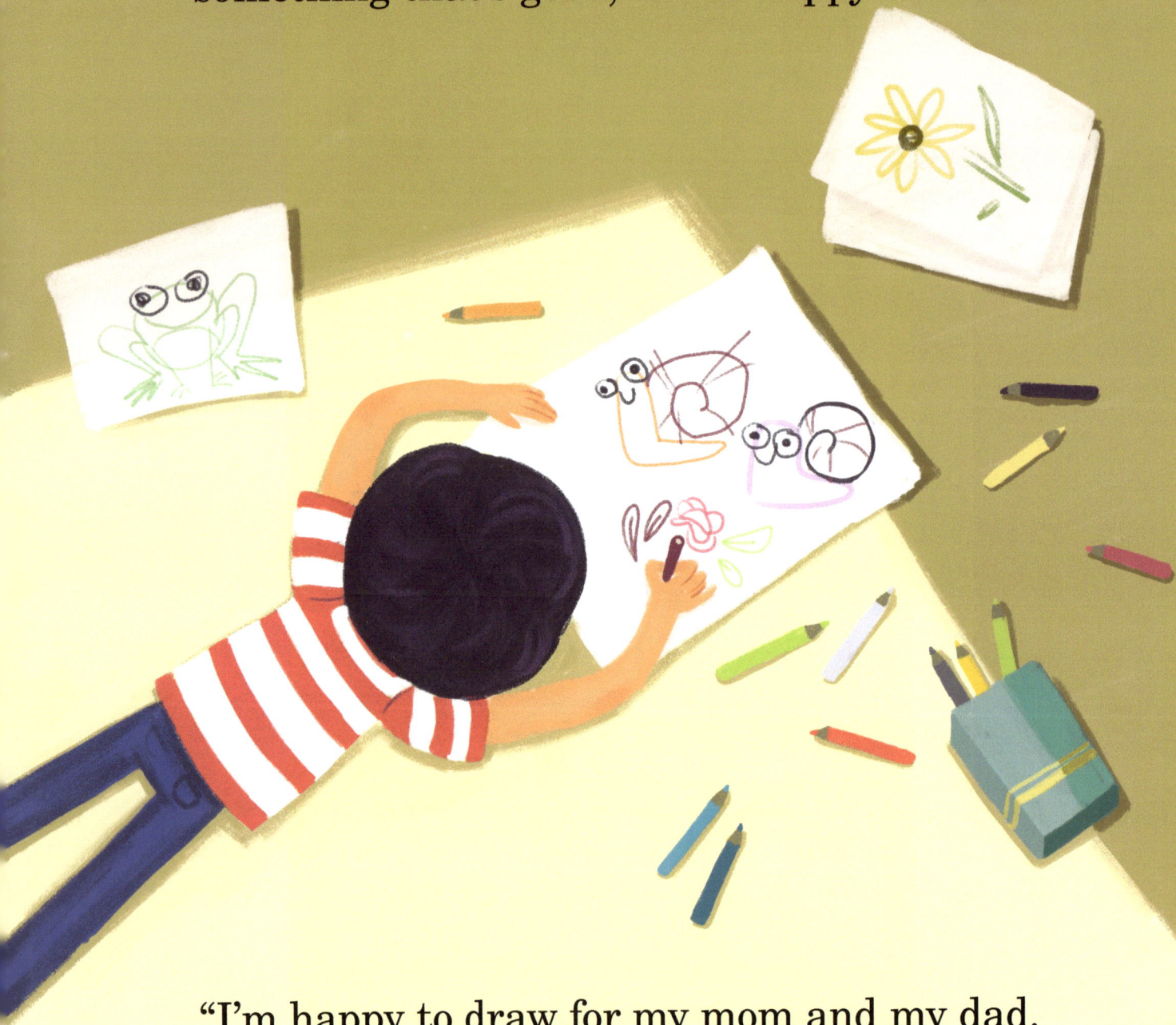

"I'm happy to draw for my mom and my dad.
I know they'll like it. It makes them feel glad."

As he's drawing his picture using colours galour.
He hears his mom say "There's some kids at the door."

"They want to know if you can come out to play."
"Yay," said the boy. "Good things come my way."

www.ingramcontent.com/pod-product-compliance
Lightning Source LLC
Chambersburg PA
CBHW042108040426

42448CB00002B/182